What Can You Ride?

Color the spaces with **I** red.
Color the spaces with **i** blue.

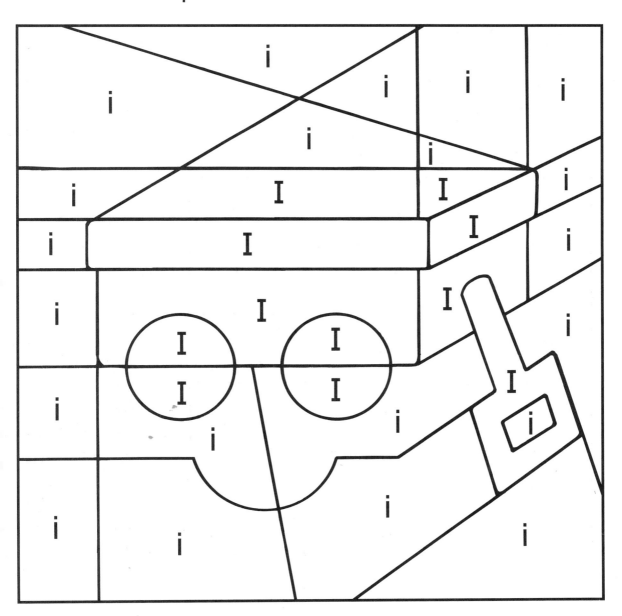

Music Maker

Color the spaces with **J** green.
Color the spaces with **j** yellow.

Sharing Time

Connect the dots from **A** to **J**. Color.

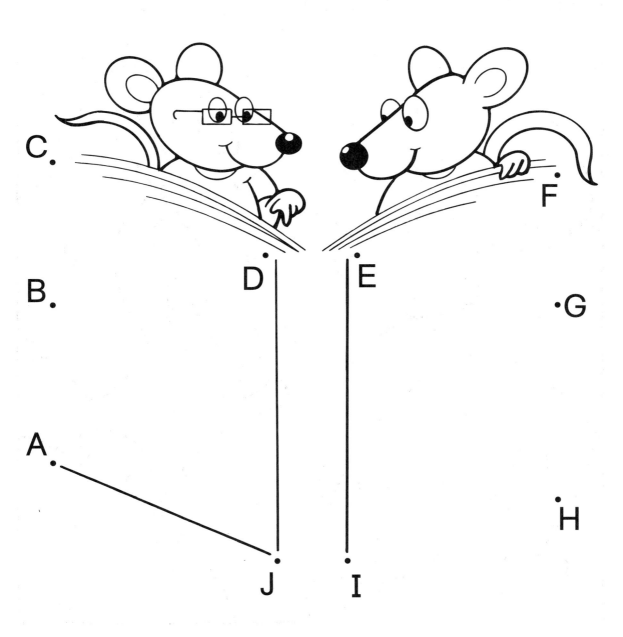

What Can Ring?

Connect the dots from **a** to **j**. Color.

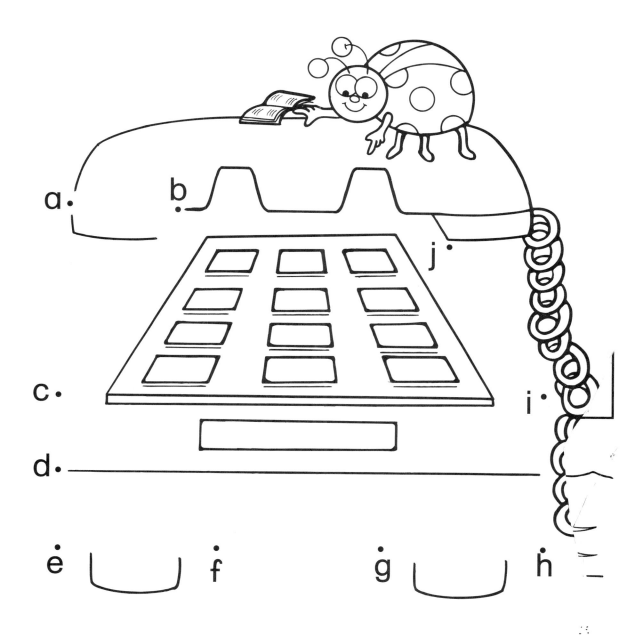

FS-11057 Alphabet Puzzles and Games

A Sea Giant

Color the spaces with **M** blue.
Color the spaces with **m** black.

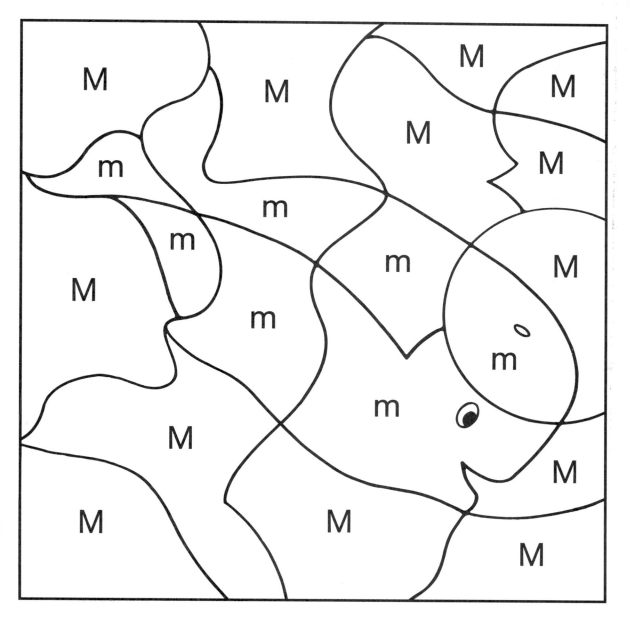

Alphabet Soup

Find the letters from **A** to **M** in the soup. Color them.

A B C D E F G H I J K L M

What Is in the Hat?

Connect the dots from **a** to **m**.
Color.

FS-11057 Alphabet Puzzles and Games

What Shines?

Color the spaces with **N** orange.
Color the spaces with **n** yellow.

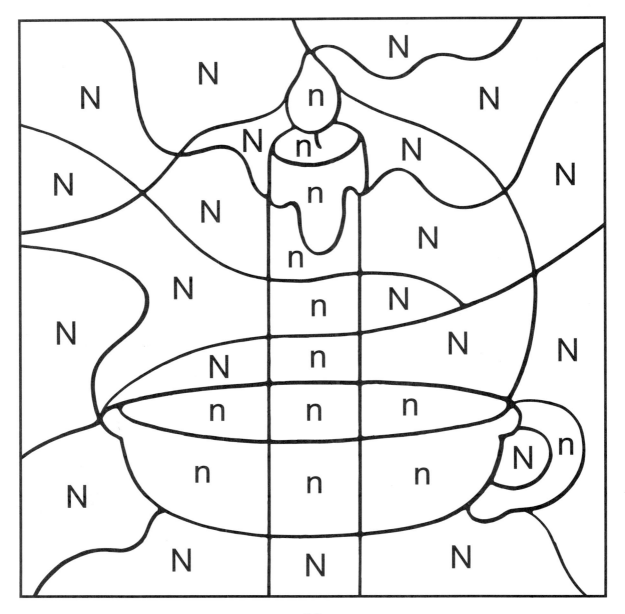

What Can Hop?

olor the spaces with **S** green.
lor the spaces with **T** yellow.

Ready for Rain

Color the spaces with **s** red.
Color the spaces with **t** blue.

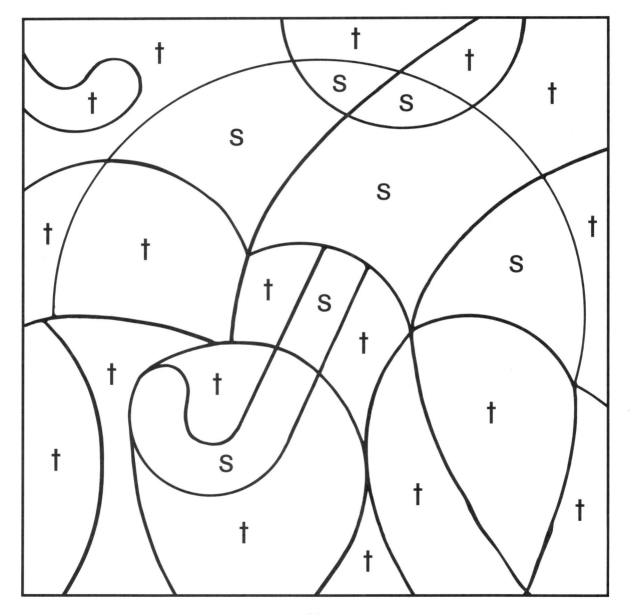

A Pretty Gift

Connect the dots from **A** to **Z**. Color.

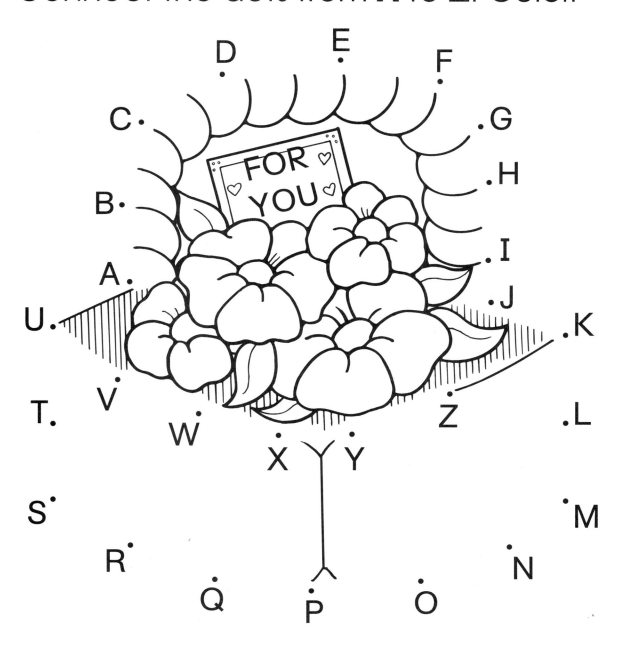

FOR YOU

FS-11057 Alphabet Puzzles and Games

Let's Explore

Connect the dots from **a** to **z**. Color.

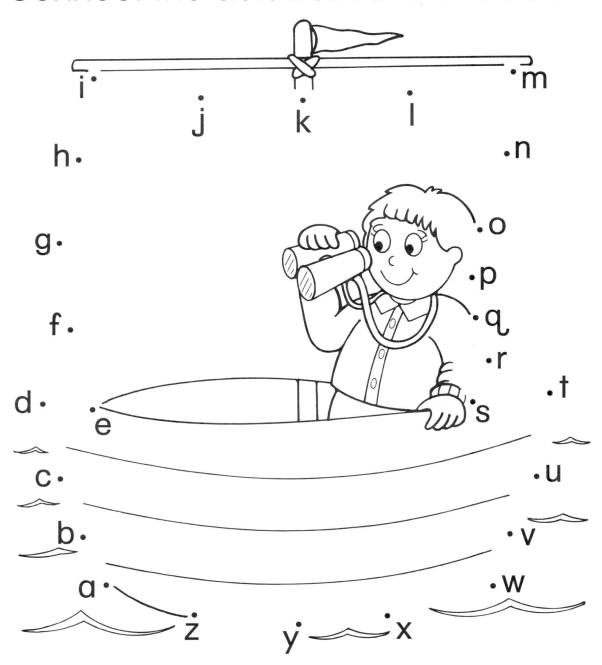

Trucking Along

To find the mystery letter, color
the spaces with these letters red.

A K M C F B L J H G D

Circle the mystery letter.   **D   E   O**

A Special Quilt

To find the mystery letter, color the spaces with these letters yellow.

i   y   a   x   h   n   t   v   u   l

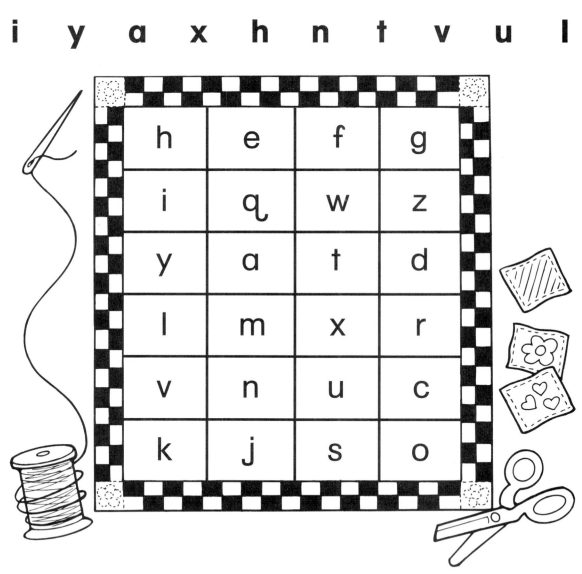

h	e	f	g
i	q	w	z
y	a	t	d
l	m	x	r
v	n	u	c
k	j	s	o

Circle the mystery letter.   **b   o   t**

What's on TV?

To find the mystery letter, color the spaces with these letters green.

V I X P E N O S M R L Z

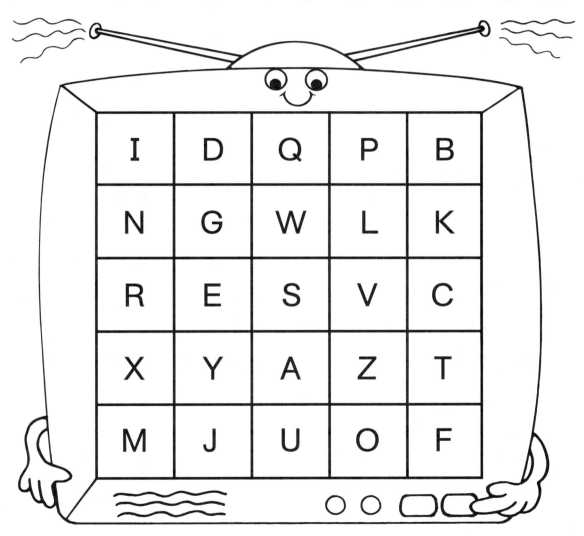

I	D	Q	P	B
N	G	W	L	K
R	E	S	V	C
X	Y	A	Z	T
M	J	U	O	F

Circle the mystery letter.   **B   T   H**

An Alphabet House

Find the mystery letter. Color the spaces with these letters blue.

b   r   i   e   k   s   u   m   t

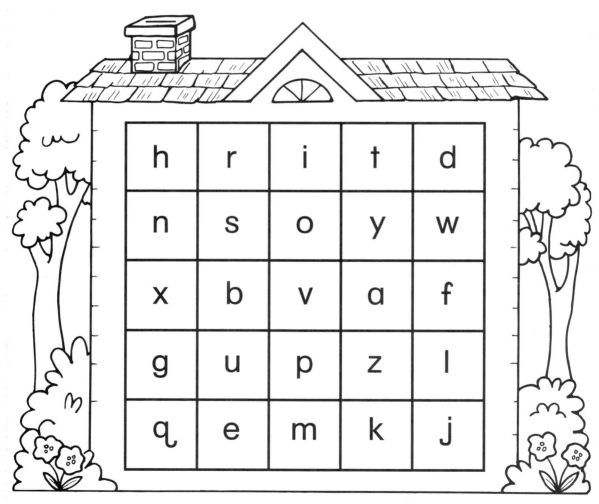

h	r	i	t	d
n	s	o	y	w
x	b	v	a	f
g	u	p	z	l
q	e	m	k	j

Circle the mystery letter.   **c   o   r**

38   FS-11057 Alphabet Puzzles and Games

A Sweet Treat

Color the spaces with **a** brown.
Color the spaces with **e** yellow.
Color the spaces with **g** orange.

A Circus Star

Color the spaces with **k** yellow.
Color the spaces with **n** black.
Color the spaces with **o** red.

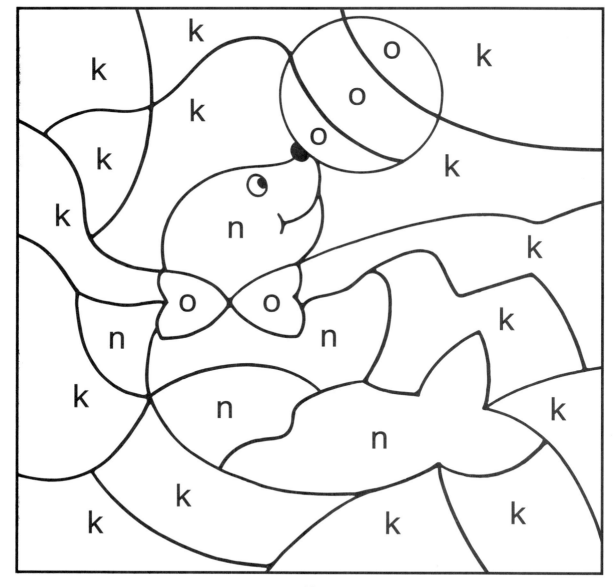

Visiting the Queen

Color each **q** in the picture orange.
Then color the rest of the picture.

Up in the Air

Color each **u** in the picture purple.
Then color the rest of the picture.

Tasty Vegetables

Color each **v** in the picture green.
Then color the rest of the picture.

Time to Get Up

Find these things that begin with **b**. Color them blue. Then color the rest of the picture.

ball   bed   bat   bike   bird

Let's Go for a Ride

Find these things that begin with **c**.
Color them red. Then color the rest of
the picture.

cup　　car　　clock　　crayon　　cat

Lunchtime

Find these things that begin with **d**. Color them yellow. Then color the rest of the picture.

doll   dog   dish   duck   door

FS-11057 Alphabet Puzzles and Games

Hard at Work

Find these things that begin with **l**. Color them orange. Then color the rest of the picture.

lamp   leaf   log   ladder   lion

FS-11057 Alphabet Puzzles and Games

What a Story!

Find these things that begin with **m**. Color them brown. Then color the rest of the picture.

mouse   milk   mop   mask   monkey

48

At the Restaurant

Find these things that begin with **p**. Color them yellow. Then color the rest of the picture.

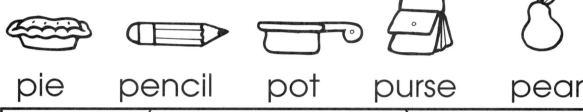

pie   pencil   pot   purse   pear

    49   FS-11057 Alphabet Puzzles and Games

A Rainy Day

Find these things that begin with **r**. Color them red. Then color the rest of the picture.

rake   ring   rocket   rope   rug

Fun in the Snow

Find these things that begin with **s**. Color them yellow. Then color the rest of the picture.

sun   saw   snake   star   sled

      51   FS-11057 Alphabet Puzzles and Games

Counting Stars

Find these things that begin with **t**. Color them blue. Then color the rest of the picture.

table   turtle   tent   towel   tape

52

All Aboard!

Connect the dots from **A** to **Z**. Color.

An Island Home

Connect the dots from **a** to **z**. Color.

     FS-11057 Alphabet Puzzles and Games

Marching Home

Make a path for the ants to get home.
Color the path in order from **A** to **Z**.

A	B	C	D
Z	O	M	E

K	J	I	H	G	F
L	F	P	M	S	P
M	I	U	V	W	A
N	F	T	D	X	C
O	B	S	E	Y	Z
P	Q	R	A		

FS-11057 Alphabet Puzzles and Games

A Night Flyer

Make a path from the owl to the tree.
Color the path in order from **a** to **z**.

a	b	c	d

h	i	o	j	e

o	n	m	l	p	f

p	k	t	k	q	g

q	g	f	j	i	h

r	b	s	r	c	d

s	e	a	x	y	z

t	u	v	w

FS-11057 Alphabet Puzzles and Games